PAINTING WITH WORDS

Edited By Lynsey Evans

First published in Great Britain in 2024 by:

Young Writers
Remus House
Coltsfoot Drive
Peterborough
PE2 9BF
Telephone: 01733 890066
Website: www.youngwriters.co.uk

Printed and bound in the UK by BookPrintingUK
Website: www.bookprintinguk.com
YB0575J

FOREWORD

For Young Writers' latest competition This Is Me,
we asked primary school pupils to look inside
themselves, to think about what makes them unique,
and then write a poem about it! They rose to the
challenge magnificently and the result is this fantastic
collection of poems in a variety of poetic styles.

Here at Young Writers our aim is to encourage creativity
in children and to inspire a love of the written word, so
it's great to get such an amazing response, with some
absolutely fantastic poems. It's important for children to
focus on and celebrate themselves and this competition
allowed them to write freely and honestly, celebrating
what makes them great, expressing their hopes and
fears, or simply writing about their favourite things.
This Is Me gave them the power of words. The result
is a collection of inspirational and moving poems that
also showcase their creativity and writing ability.

I'd like to congratulate all the young poets
in this anthology, I hope this inspires them
to continue with their creative writing.

CONTENTS

Ralphy Lett (8)	56
Carol Ellis (8)	57
Rory Hughes (8)	58
Martin Oliver (8)	59
Halle Woolacott (8)	60
Ollie Taylor (8)	61
Skyla Griffin (8)	62
Nancy Marie Eastwood (9)	63
Pearl-Blossom Lee (9)	64
Halli Hitch (8)	65
Francesca Parham (8)	66
Violet Griffin (7)	67
Chloe Clarke (8)	68
Charlotte Finch (8)	69
Freddie (8)	70
Olly Dempsey (8)	71
Matilda Pettit (8)	72
Harrison Ashdown (8)	73
William Badham (8)	74
Daniella De Bourbon (8)	75
Hannah Osenton (8)	76
Jemima Larkin (8)	77

Knockmore Primary School, Lisburn

Jaya Pall (9)	78
Jared Corbett (8)	79
Jo Ferguson (8)	80
Summer Hines-Pugh (9)	81

Knocknagor Primary School, Trillick

Kyla Grainger (10)	82
Oisín Keenan (10)	83
Finn Maguire (10)	84
Ronan McCaffrey (9)	85

Lever Edge Primary Academy, Bolton

Guyatu Abdullahi (10)	86

Newton Primary School, Newton

Poppy Lloyd (11)	88
Jake Billingsley (8)	89
Jess Giles (10)	90
Isabelle Emm (10)	92
Oliver Dodd (10)	93
Zach Kennah (10)	94
Jake Mylchreest (8)	95
Katie Spellman (10)	96
Marco Stather (11)	97
Scarlett Lennon (8)	98
Naya Elmenshawy (8)	99
Kate Giles (10)	100
Kallie Vincent (8)	101
Rowan Cornwell (8)	102
Dylan Shaw (10)	103
Freddy Armstrong (10)	104
Sumaiya Khan (10)	105
Lucy Hodson (8)	106
Idris Thomas (9)	107
Aiyla Stamp (8)	108
Scott Cornwell (11)	109
Poppy-Ella Coathup Pinches (8)	110
Jacob Heap (10)	111
Elliot Shaw (8)	112
Alice Crimp (9)	113
Josh Barlow Ashworth (8)	114
Zara Ates (8)	115
Oluwalolope Femi-Pius (10)	116
Imani Uddin (8)	117
Poppy Tromans (8)	118
Sameena Uddin (8)	119
Dahlia Walsh (8)	120
James Hodson	121
Arthur March (10)	122
Ben Cooper (9)	123
Molly Lee (8)	124
Ethan Powell (8)	125
James Shennan (8)	126
Rosemae Armstrong (8)	127
Jos Hearse (10)	128
Daniel Georgiev (8)	129
Benjamin Foxton (8)	130

Saif Uddin 131
Lily Otton (8) 132
Orla Lloyd (8) 133
Alexander Robertshaw- 134
Lewis (10)
Jennifer-Rose Thompson (8) 135
Francesca Mylchreest (10) 136
George Dodd (8) 137
Pippa Jackson (8) 138
Alfred Evans-Wood (10) 139
Cerys Malone (9) 140
Evie Docking (9) 141
Edward Boyce (10) 142
Elizabeth Wall (10) 143
Frank Ivory (8) 144
Martha Storey (10) 145
Zimal Baiq (8) 146
Aoibheann Gunessee (10) 147
Jacob Lewis (8) 148
Daisy Roberts (10) 149
Liyana Haque (10) 150
Bella Brown (11) 151
Juni Ivory (10) 152
Hank Starck (10) 153

North Lancing Primary School, Lancing

Ida Ainsworth-Ballinger (9) 154

Pennine Way Junior Academy, Swadlincote

Joshua Bell (7) 155
Grace Vorley (10) 156
Martha Topley (8) 158
Clara McGill (7) 159
Faith Smith (9) 160
Billie-Rae Mack (8) 161
Lily-Rose Evans (8) 162
Lilia Ruston (9) 163
Danielle Sharp (10) 164
Abbie-Jo Collier (8) 165
Ryan Inight (8) 166

Laciee Mitchener (7) 167
Amelia Dyke (7) 168

Rockmount Primary School, Upper Norwood

Amelie Wong (8) 169
Audrey Neil (7) 170
Amber Bartle (7) 171
Gabriel Shapcott (8) 172
Amir Douglas (7) 173
Miles E Peters (7) 174
Frank Wilson (7) 175

Sion Mills Primary School, Sion Mills

Lauren Galloway-Doherty (10) 176
Riley McNamee (11) 178
Tom Hyndman 179
Aoife Kelly (10) 180
Mia Bradley (10) 181
Ollie Millar 182
Alex Patterson (10) 183
Lincoln Harpur (10) 184
Maya Catterson (10) 185
Holly Moore (10) 186
Jayne Annesley 187
Oliver Williamson (10) 188
Cara Brown (10) 189
Farrah Crompton-Pattison (10) 190
Kamile Elijosiute (11) 191
Gracey Hamilton (10) 192
Tom Freeborn 193
Ellie Magee (11) 194
Alyssia Calvert (10) 195
Keelim Moore (10) 196
Patrick Colhoun 197
Harry Adams (10) 198

Southway Primary School, Bognor Regis

Hannah Dowle (9)	199
Sofia Delieu-Gaitan (9)	200
Anna Barthik (7)	201

St Matthew's CE Primary School, West Wimbledon

Matthew Rankin (8)	202
Edward Jarman (8)	203
Senara Bacon (8)	204
Izabella Scheerova (8)	205
Raphael Faponnle (8)	206
Larissa De Campos-Michalowicz (8)	207
Calla Bliss Rayne (8)	208
Freya Tamblyn (9)	209

St Teresa's Catholic Primary School, Parkfields

Holiness Amfo Nkrumab (7)	210
Chikaima Ezekaka (7)	211
Meagan Mazivanhanga (7)	212
Ketochi Okenwa (7)	213
Tajveer Kang (7)	214
Talisha Linton (7)	215
Marcus Nagy (7)	216
Amelia Mehmi (7)	217
Enoch Shittu (7)	218
Kendrick Dyoco (8)	219
Lailena Madden	220
Krishiv Sharma (8)	221
Hasel Usieki (7)	222
David Lawal (7)	223
Sara Williams (7)	224
Tyrell Madden (7)	225

Whinhill Primary School, Greenock

Millie McKay (9)	226
Owen Porteous (9)	227

Thomas Robertson (7)	228
Ajay Mohan (8)	229
Evan Smillie (8)	230
Cameron Marshall (9)	231
Kameron Morrison (8)	232
Jake Barclay (8)	233
Noah Doherty (8)	234
Macey Quigg (9)	235
Evie Jamieson (9)	236
Ikram Mashwani (9)	237
Kian O'Shea (9)	238
Blake McKinnon (9)	239

Ysgol Gymraeg Henllan, Henllan

Hannah Muhammad (10)	240
Jacob Roberts (9)	241
Efa Parkes (10)	242
Molly Lawson (10)	243
Leah Jones (10)	244
Noa Evans (10)	245
Ifan Hughes (9)	246
Azzaam Muhammad (9)	247
Elizabeth Vaughan Hepple (10)	248
Neville Headley (9)	249
Elis Smith (10)	250
Harvey Davies (11)	251
Cenwyn Arman (9)	252
Megan J (9)	253
Scarlett Jones (10)	254

THE POEMS

This Is Me

So, you have asked me who I am,
Well, let me tell you,
This is me.

I am an adventurous monkey,
Jumping around, playing games,
This is me.

But, I am also a dolphin,
Swimming in pools, playing in the depths,
This is me.

And I'm a dog,
Forgetting my training, missing half,
This is me.

I'm as nosy as an eagle,
Prowling around, scanning the skies,
This is me.

As lazy as a lizard,
Sitting around all day, waiting to warm,
This is me.

Emma Newberry (9)
Alvechurch CE Middle School, Alvechurch

Indi's World!

It's hard to list all the things I love to do,
But for a start, here are a few:

Baking biscuits is good fun, but I have to hide
some so Daddy doesn't eat them!

I love to dance, especially in shows,
All the costumes and twirling on my toes.

I have lots of friends from different places,
It's so much fun to catch up and see their faces.

But let me finish with the best;
Of course, it's horses, better than all the rest!

Indi Deakin (9)
Alvechurch CE Middle School, Alvechurch

Parts Of Me

H ope is something that keeps high in low times

A ims and goals keep me going, never a dull day in my life

P eople I love keep me strong and encourage me

P erseverance, never give up, carry on no matter how hard

Y ears have gone by, and I'm still strong.

M e and my friends are never going to give up

E volution is something that happens every day.

Susie Mullen (10)
Alvechurch CE Middle School, Alvechurch

The Gymnast

The gymnast hurling through the air
We were screaming because there
Was something flying in the air!

Amy reached up to the sky
And she flew onto a parachute
And was riding the parachute.

Poppy Morgan (9)
Alvechurch CE Middle School, Alvechurch

Perfect Chaos

J umbly thoughts but so many skills.

A ncient history is so great.

C reating Lego masterpieces calms my storm.

K nowledge is power and my power is my differences.

Jack James (9)
Alvechurch CE Middle School, Alvechurch

It's About Me

D elightful, delightful, delightful.
A m always happy and cheerful.
N arrating stories is my favourite.
N ew things make me happy, a bit.

J oining a new group of people makes me shy.
O h, I love to see birds fly.

F ixing things makes me proud of myself.
R iding a bicycle is the only activity I like for myself.
A ppreciating others' qualities is a thing I like about me.
N owadays, I love new places I see.
C reating crafts is my hobby,
I also love to do things joyfully.
S o, now you know who I am.

Dann Jo Francis (11)
Brentry Primary School, Bristol

Trapped

Someone screaming in your ear
Someone drowning you
Anxiety and fear.

Someone locking the door
When you just want to be home
Trees closing in on you, making it worse.

Someone taking your confidence
And draining your happiness
Life feels impossible, waves take over.

You wish you weren't like this
But someone says you have to be.

Everything happening all at once
Need to move, you can't breathe
But you wonder who is that someone?

It's a tiny person in your head, making things up
You are safe
So, *don't give up.*

Eliza Matthews (9)
Brentry Primary School, Bristol

The Funny Clowns

The clowns are honking, talking, saying
funny jokes.
Tricks and tricks all over the place.
Jumping up and down.
Balancing on big, tall ropes, they are very talented.
How about you?
They are honking, talking, saying funny jokes.
They have a clown festival every year.
Even at Brentry Primary, the best school ever.
I love this school, even their tricks are so cool.
We get wet as well.
But I don't like getting too wet at the end.

Evie Terrett (7)
Brentry Primary School, Bristol

The Trees

The trees are swaying side to side,
Sometimes, I feel like I just might cry,
Not in a sad way, only in a happy way
Because the trees are more than pretty,
More than love and more than rhyme.

They give you life, that's how we survive,
Without them, we will *die!*
So that's why we have to thank the trees
for everything,
Everything, anything and more,
So thank you very much.

Alfie Evans (10)
Brentry Primary School, Bristol

Love

Love is full of hugs and kisses.
When he leaves, you will miss him.
Love is here, love is there, love is in the air.
You might never feel loved, but I'm sure
someone loves you above.
You can love a mum, dad, brother, sister,
cat, dog, a Mrs or a Mr
You don't always need someone, you might
need something.
You might love a god, you might love a colour,
you might love another.

Grace Vallis-Ridler (9)
Brentry Primary School, Bristol

Friends

We need friends
To play with
To tease with
To share with
What would we do
If we had no friends?
Help me to think
Of countries
And think of...
Our children separating
From their family
Do they have food?
Think of this
Beautiful school
With many children
And adults
So that is why
We need friends.

Lexi Morgan (9)
Brentry Primary School, Bristol

Different!

People say hi or hey,
But sometimes I say hurray.
I love the colour pink.
I love to drink water.
I also love pandas.
I love to draw and I'm not very tall.
I make people laugh, which is a fact.
I am also very cheerful.
I love to sing and dance.
That is me.

Pandora Mills (10)
Brentry Primary School, Bristol

My Life!

I love football, I love sport,
I love playing, I love gaming,
I love reading, I like maths,
I like English, I love my family,
I love pizza, I love kebabs,
I love tea, I love Yorkshire pudding,
I love roller coasters, I love weekends,
And I love the UK.

Szymon Kazimierczuk
Brentry Primary School, Bristol

A Poem About Hugs

Hugs are warm, hugs are nice
Sometimes you need a hug
And that's alright
Snuggle, huggle, snug like a bug
Everyone I know loves a hug
Big warm arms wrapping around me
I know there's nowhere else
I'd rather be.

Ivy Vallis-Ridler (7)
Brentry Primary School, Bristol

There Is Me

My dad is English and my mum is Japanese
But an eight-year-old boy is all everyone sees
But there is much more
Even though you may think there's nothing
to look for
Then you'll see
There is me.

I may not be into most sports
But the thought of not swimming or karate haunts
I may not look like much
But there is magic in my touch
And if you still think that then you'll see
There is me.

I'm a chameleon, magical and mysterious
Going in and out in a hush
I'm always very free
Like a leaf falling from a tree
Even if the only thing you can see is me.
Then...
There is still me.

Taku Suzuki Blathwayt (8)
Brindishe Green Primary School, Hither Green

I Am Everything

I am everything,
To my Scottish family,
My nans to my grandads, to my aunties
and my uncles,
Up in Dundee,
I want to see them at least once,
It's a place in my heart,
It has a history with me,
This is me, I am everything.

I am everything,
I hate the dark,
When the lights go out, I fear a villain
is going to pop out,
It makes it hard to sleep,
But it makes me, me,
I'm everything.

I am everything
I love video games
Winning the World Cup in FIFA
Crossing the finish line first in Mario Kart

That's what makes me happy
When I get home, I want them
But my mum says, "No, empty your bag!"
That's what makes me, me
I am everything.

I am everything
From the South
I am South London
Safe streets, rocky train tracks
This is me
I am everything.

I am everything
I want to be a footballer
I am an Arsenal FC fan
It's my dream
This is me, I am everything.

Arthur Cronin (8)

Brindishe Green Primary School, Hither Green

These Are All The Things About Me

I am so good, don't you see?
I am always playful.
And also, I am always joyful.
No one is more entertained than me.
But I am very funny.
And I love being happy.
I am always shining like the stars.
I am so strong that I can lift bars.
Getting a football cup will be surprising.
Going to the beach seems exciting.
I also like travelling.
I like travelling to India on a plane.
I like playing board games.
I wish I had two homes.
But I hate garden gnomes.
I am so brave I can jump off a diving board
that is ten meters high.
And sometimes I'm really shy.

Saswin Yogenthiran (8)
Brindishe Green Primary School, Hither Green

Christmas With Family

Christmas with family
Makes me happy
We have fun together
No matter the weather
We eat the Christmas cake
that my mum lovingly bakes
My dad gets the tree
All the way from Lee
We hang up the lights
They flash so bright
My gran comes round
She always gives us a pound
When it's all done
And we've had all the fun
We collect the Christmas tree stumps
And in the boot, they go bump
Watching them in the fire burn
Waiting for next Christmas to return.

Margo Forster (8)
Brindishe Green Primary School, Hither Green

Ingredients For Me

You will need these to make me:
A wolf,
A flame,
A pufferfish,
A Scottish flag.

First, you place two wolves in my ribcage.
Next, place a flame for my temper and attention and to control my burning.
After, place a pufferfish in my belly for no reason at all, or maybe to be silly.
Finally, place a Scottish flag in my heart, where the wolves will guard it.
These are the ingredients for me.

Lex Forrester-Barlow (8)
Brindishe Green Primary School, Hither Green

Me

I love monsters, they are so cool.
In my head, monsters rule!
I am creative, I love art.
In some ways, everything finds a place in my heart.
I am curious, I want to know more.
Of everything, I want to be sure.
I am one with the world, I want to stop
global warming.
So nature can carry on forming.
I am undiscovered, I don't know all of me.
Nobody knows who I want to be.

Milo Kilty (8)
Brindishe Green Primary School, Hither Green

Love Me

I am me, I love my family,
I love doing bikes and gymnastics,
Reading and writing are my speciality.

I am me, I am grateful,
I love Sundays,
I also love rest days,
Travelling is for me.

I am different, but I don't care,
I'm not afraid to share,
'Cause that's what makes me, me,
And I know I'm different to he and she,
Love, me.

Romilly Coates (8)
Brindishe Green Primary School, Hither Green

All About Me

I am as smart, as a dictionary.
I just hate armpits, so hairy!
Who in the world hates animals?
I just love them all!
I am a proud and generous lion!
I am only afraid of touching an iron.
I am as bright as the sun in the sky.
I won't lie, sometimes I am shy.
I am calm.
I am brave.
I am kind.
I am sad.
I am angry.
I am creative.
I am me!

Zara Nguembou Kounchou (9)
Brindishe Green Primary School, Hither Green

This Is Me

I am
A beaming star in the moonlight
As funny as a clown fighting
A silly sausage
I reflect the sun with my beauty
This is me
I am as strong as an elephant holding a tree
I am as fast as a cheetah
I take as long as a snail to get ready in the
morning
I will always like Taylor Swift
But most importantly
I like me
This is me.

Poppy Sheterline (9)
Brindishe Green Primary School, Hither Green

To Make Me

To make me,
You can't be mean, only kind.
Look inside me and my love you will find.

To make me,
You need to love to read,
And be full of curiosity.

To make me,
You need to be silly,
Creative, funny and fancy.

To make me,
Your heart should be warm, not chilly.
Full of love and witty.

Kellis Boakye (9)
Brindishe Green Primary School, Hither Green

This Is What Makes Me, Me

I am strong like an elephant pulling a tree out
of the ground.
I am proud, like a lion sitting on the rock lazily.
I am silly, like a sausage sizzling on the barbeque.
I am funny like a clown squeaking its red nose.
I am beautiful, like shiny jewellery reflecting in
the light.
This is what makes me, me.

Isabella Nicoli (9)

Brindishe Green Primary School, Hither Green

Family Support

I hate people
Not having freedom
I say enough of
Not giving people freedom
Seeing all of my old memories
Make me happy
Me and my family love each other
The same quality
Ending this is hard
But I want to tell you one last thing
'Cause, this is me.

Sophia Zafani (8)
Brindishe Green Primary School, Hither Green

Love Me

Dear me
I am grateful for what I have
Please keep hugging and reading
Try to be happy
You make me read like a falcon
You make me as fast as a cheetah
And as flexible as a jaguar
You help me, you give me hope
Love me.

Diego Quadrano (9)
Brindishe Green Primary School, Hither Green

About Me

A mazing child.

B rave at being in the wild.

O bsessed with cats.

U ses lots of equations to do maths.

T ests new stuff.

M y games are never rough.

E verything can be fun!

Alia Sameem (9)

Brindishe Green Primary School, Hither Green

My Twin

T ogether from birth
W e are fierce like tigers
I n this world, we will be together for nearly our whole lives
N o one can separate us!

Albert Cronin (8)

Brindishe Green Primary School, Hither Green

Crayon Poem

Hi, my name is Blue,
I've seen you in the crew,
You see me for the view,
And you always say it's true!
My best friend is Green,
She always uses the screen,
So she's a sassy queen.
Her not-so-best friend is Pink,
She always uses ink,
Pink gets very chatty when she gets a fresh nappy!

Saanvi Jha (8)
Drove Primary School, Swindon

Planes

I saw a plane in Colombo,
It was a jumbo.
I thought, *Where can I go?*
Can I sit in cargo?
I thought the cargo was going to Glasgow,
But instead, it went to Chicago!
I ate a burrito,
But it had tomato.
One of the crew whose name was Jake,
He gave me a slice of cake.
Just when I was drooling,
I had a dream of hiking.
When we came on approach,
I saw a roach.
I wanted to go to America,
But it ended up being Costa Rica.
I saw a flight simulator,
I thought, *can I do it later?*
When the turbulence came,

I thought I was ending up in an ambulance.
Finally, I reached where I wanted,

Thank God my flight was not haunted!

Neil Pitke (8)
Drove Primary School, Swindon

This Is Me

What makes me special?
What makes me, me?
Is my good heart and quality?
Black is my hair,
Brown are my eyes.
I am eight years old,
I am very bold.
My name is Radhika and as you can see,
I'm happy to be me!
My hands are for helping,
My heart is for caring,
This is my body and I love all of me.
When I laugh,
I make people happy.
When I smile,
I light up the room.
I love my pets,
I give them respect.
I have a vegetarian diet,
Because killing animals to eat is not right.
Hinduism is my religion,

It teaches me no discrimination.
I am smart and I have a kind heart,
This is my life and I am happy to be me.

Radhika Shrivastawa (8)
Drove Primary School, Swindon

Stars

Stars are red, stars are blue
Stars are all colours, except for you
Stars are bright, stars are nice
But they always go away because of you
I like stars, I like night
So you always have to say thank you
Stars make me sleep, stars make me brave
And that's why I snore, night, night!
I hope you liked my star poem
Don't forget to say night-night!

Meeqaat Adam (8)
Drove Primary School, Swindon

This Is Me

This is me,
Yes, the lovely, jolly me,
The me who likes reading and painting,
This is me,
The me is kind,
Who also is a sweetheart,
This is me,
Of course, one has to be smart,
For little crafts,
This is me,
I dream about being adventurous,
Sometimes a little bit curious,
This is me!

Aashvi Singh (8)
Drove Primary School, Swindon

From The Window, I Can See

From the window
I can see
Two birds fighting together
In a tree.

From the window
I can see
The sun smiling
Brightly at me.

From the window
I can see
All the animals
Staring at me.

From the window
I can see
All the people
Waving at me.

Ayumi Shanbhag (8)
Drove Primary School, Swindon

Myself

My name is very sweet
I like to hear birds tweet
I love to read
I also like a drum beat
I like smelling flowers
Play, sing, dance and run
I love the sea
I love the seashells
I love sand
I like ice cream
I love everything
I am proud to be me.

Thisumlee Usarambage (9)
Drove Primary School, Swindon

Poppies

Gardens full of poppies,
We honour the brave,
Who are now in their graves

These are the men who fought
hard to keep you safe,
Now it's your turn to remember the engrave.

Thank you!

Aara Wagh (8)
Drove Primary School, Swindon

Friends

F riends make me happy

R especting each other

I mportant to me

E very day we play together

N ever make me feel sad

D ecide things together

S pecial in life.

Novak Fernandes (9)

Drove Primary School, Swindon

This Is Me

A bee bringing pollen to his hive.
The bee ate it and it was good.
Suddenly, a boy took it.
The bee was angry and stung the boy.
He was sad.
I am scared when it's dark.
We are playing together.
I am trying to play with my friends.
I am creative and excited.
I am as fast as a ball to be played.

I am angry like a teacher.
I am bored like a flower when a bee goes to it.
This is my poem.
I was jealous when a girl took my toy.
I am annoyed when there is too much music.
I am me.

Riley Lawrence (7)
Eastway Primary School, Wirral

Untitled

I am scared.
I am anxious like a pencil that got broken.
I am powerless when I can't do something.
I am overwhelmed like a ruler.
I am me.
I am angry.
I am bored when there's nothing to do.
I am jealous when I don't have something.
I am annoyed like a leaf.
I am me.
I am happy.
I am caring like a cute, cuddly penguin.
I am grateful when I get new things.
I am excited like a garden in the summer.
I am me.

Kian Davies (7)
Eastway Primary School, Wirral

This Is Me

I am happy.

I am grateful for the world behind me.

I am caring for my family and friends.

I am excited about dancing.

I am me.

I am sad.

I am hurt when the rain falls.

I am lonely without my teddies.

I am disappointed when I am away from Mum.

I am me.

I am angry.

I am jealous when my cousin gets a PS5.

I am annoyed like a fossil in a rock.

I am bored like a chair that can't move.

I am me.

Isla Howell (7)

Eastway Primary School, Wirral

This Is Me

I am playful
I am creative like a picture
I am curious when someone keeps
a secret from me
I am affectionate
I am me.

I am sad
I am lonely like a feather blowing in the wind
I am hurt when no one is with me
I am disappointed when it's raining
I am me.

I am happy
I am caring like a polar bear helping his mum
I am grateful for everyone
I am excited for birthdays
I am me.

Stacey Douglas (7)
Eastway Primary School, Wirral

Untitled

I am loved.
I am respected like a flower to a bee.
I am valued 'cause my friends are kind.
I am me.

I am happy.
I care for people because I am caring.
I am grateful for getting candy at Halloween.
I am excited like a puppy jumping.
I am me.

I am scared like KFC chicken wings.
I am powerless like a rock.
I am dead like an anxious body.
I am overwhelmed when I clean up.
I am me.

Lottie-Jo Cassidy
Eastway Primary School, Wirral

Untitled

I am creative like scissors.
I am curious when I talk about movies.
I am affectionate when I win a football match.
I am me.
I am bored when it is a Sunday.
I am jealous when I go to my friends' houses.
I am annoyed when I lose in football.
I am me.
I am lonely when my mum and dad go to the
petrol station.
I am hurt when I get slide-tackled.
I am disappointed like a flower in the winter.
I am me.

Ollie Jones (7)
Eastway Primary School, Wirral

I Am Me

I am happy.
I am caring and like being people's friends.
I am grateful like a plant getting water.
I am excited like the light.
I am me.

I am sad.
I am hurt when I lose someone.
I am lonely like the sea.
I am disappointed when I lose a game.
I am me.

I am playful.
I am creative like a whiteboard.
I am curious like a cat.
I am affectionate like a teddy bear.
I am me.

Zak Lunt (7)
Eastway Primary School, Wirral

This Is Me

I am happy like a teacher.
I am loved like my mum.
I am grateful for the summer hot dogs.
I am powerful when I go to the gym.
I am as brave as a cheetah.
I am excited when I get a surprise.
I am me.

I am sad like a broken-down tree.
I am hurt when I crash my Ferrari.
I am annoyed when I have no money.
I am bored when a pebble is sitting.
And a person comes over to my face.
I am me.

Reggie Birch (7)
Eastway Primary School, Wirral

Untitled

I am loved.
I am respected like a bee making honey.
I am valued by my friends.
I am accepted for doing what I do.
I am me.

I am happy.
I am caring to others.
I am excited like a kitten.
I am grateful for what I have.
I am me.

I am sad.
I am lonely like a rainbow in the sky.
I am hurt when I fall over.
I am disappointed when I don't get sweets.
I am me.

Aideen Henry (7)
Eastway Primary School, Wirral

Untitled

I am happy.
I am caring like a heart.
I am grateful for every one.
I am excited like the swings.
I am me.

I am angry.
I am bored like a lighthouse.
I am jealous of people's things.
I am annoyed by screaming in the house.
I am me.

I am playful.
I am creative like a plant.
I am curious like a dog.
I am affectionate like a teddy bear.
I am me.

Trinity White (7)

Eastway Primary School, Wirral

I Am Me

I am sad.
I am happy.
I am lonely like a fossil.
I am caring.
I am loved.
I am me.
I am bored like a fossil on the beach.
I am lonely like a bee following a group of people.
I am as mad as a big sister about to go on a
night out.
I am overwhelmed as if I am a big leaf falling
from a tree.
I am me.

Ella-Rose Randles (8)
Eastway Primary School, Wirral

A Poem All About Me

M agnificent

E ndless

L ovely little girl

I f you're in trouble, she is there

S cientific

S uper

A ny trouble yet?

S tyle!

P riceless hero

O n the move

E veryone can rely on her

M ore saving to do.

Melissa Ross (8)

High Halstow Primary School, High Halstow

My Favourite Sport

I ce

L aughter
O utstanding at football
V aluable
E xtreme

H ockey
O utstanding
C razy
K nowledgable
E xcited
Y es, ice hockey is the best.

Franky Faggetter (8)
High Halstow Primary School, High Halstow

Myself And My Personality

O ne and only.

U nique.

T echnology.

S ushi.

T abby cats.

A migo.

N ever ever naughty.

D ecent at cooking.

I love cats.

N umber one girl.

G irls rule!

Mya Hewitt-Schembri (8)
High Halstow Primary School, High Halstow

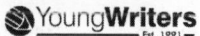

Like A Cheetah

R elaxing
E xcellent
A cceptable
L aughing
L ikable
Y es, I like running

F riendly
A bsolutely amazing at football
S o smiley
T errific runner.

Ralphy Lett (8)
High Halstow Primary School, High Halstow

Myself

A dorable and cute

M agnificent horse rider

A stonishing girly girl

Z en, *hum, hum, hum, hum*

I maginative person

N ever ever give up

G enerous at everything.

Carol Ellis (8)
High Halstow Primary School, High Halstow

My Favourite Football Team

L eague title race
I ntrigued
V ariable
E xcellent at maths
R ap master
P ink is my favourite colour
O pen-minded
O ptimistic
L ast-minute super save.

Rory Hughes (8)
High Halstow Primary School, High Halstow

All About Me

A mazing to others,
L oving,
L iverpool.

A wesome,
B rainy,
O utstanding,
U nique,
T ennis.

M agnificent,
E xtraordinary.

Martin Oliver (8)
High Halstow Primary School, High Halstow

Kind

F anta
U nique
N o cats
N o kittens
Y ou are amazing

M usic lover
A pple hater
K ind
E aster adorer
R are.

Halle Woolacott (8)

High Halstow Primary School, High Halstow

Liverpool

L azy

I ntelligent

V ery talented at football

E ight

R eally likes football

P andas

O utstanding

O ne and only

L aughter.

Ollie Taylor (8)
High Halstow Primary School, High Halstow

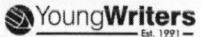

Gymnastics

G enius
Y oga talented
M agical
N aughty
A stonishing
S tretchy
T iny
I ncredible
C aring
S uper cool skills.

Skyla Griffin (8)
High Halstow Primary School, High Halstow

Magical Me

B FF
E xcellent
S tar
T earful

F orgetful
R eflective
I ntelligent
E xcited
N ever gives up
D one.

Nancy Marie Eastwood (9)
High Halstow Primary School, High Halstow

This Is Me

L oves her dogs
O nly one of me
V ery good listener
E verybody's friend
L oves everybody
Y um! That is what I say when I eat ice cream.

Pearl-Blossom Lee (9)

High Halstow Primary School, High Halstow

This Is Me

A mazing

N ever gives up

I ntelligent

M agnificent

A bsolutely loves the sea

L aughter

S miles every day.

Halli Hitch (8)

High Halstow Primary School, High Halstow

All About Me

T he best
H appy
I ntelligent
S weet

I mpatient
S uper

M yself
E very day.

Francesca Parham (8)
High Halstow Primary School, High Halstow

Horse

H i, my name is Violet

O ptimistic learner

R oses are my favourite flower

S eafood is the best

E very horse is my friend.

Violet Griffin (7)

High Halstow Primary School, High Halstow

This Is Me

L oves to play
O pen minded
V ery good communicator
I nquirer in everything
N ever gives up
G reat at maths.

Chloe Clarke (8)
High Halstow Primary School, High Halstow

This Is Me

C onfident

A n excellent listener

R esponsible

I ncredible

N ice like a little girl on her birthday

G enius.

Charlotte Finch (8)

High Halstow Primary School, High Halstow

Football Fanatic

F riend

O rdinary

O utstanding

T hrilling

B est friend

A nimal

L oyalty

L ively.

Freddie (8)

High Halstow Primary School, High Halstow

Kitten Poem

K ittens are cute.

I 'm a cat lover.

T abby cats are cool.

T errfic me.

E normous brain.

N o dogs.

Olly Dempsey (8)

High Halstow Primary School, High Halstow

Myself

M yself, Matilda,
Y ou are amazing,
S mily,
E xtraordinary,
L ove acrostic poems,
F antastic.

Matilda Pettit (8)
High Halstow Primary School, High Halstow

This Is Me

W ell behaved

E xcellent

S mart

T alented

H appy

A mazing

M agnificent.

Harrison Ashdown (8)

High Halstow Primary School, High Halstow

Gaming Me!

G ame star

A mazing

M agnificent

I ntelligent

N ight gamer

G asps when losing a game!

William Badham (8)

High Halstow Primary School, High Halstow

This Is Me

Young learner
Beautiful looking
Loves singing
Smart thinker
Amazing artist
Exciting talents.

Daniella De Bourbon (8)

High Halstow Primary School, High Halstow

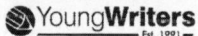

Happy Days

H appy

A mazing

P ink

P retty

Y ou're a superstar.

Hannah Osenton (8)

High Halstow Primary School, High Halstow

My Favourite Animal

B eautiful

U nique

N ice

N aughty

Y oung.

Jemima Larkin (8)

High Halstow Primary School, High Halstow

All About Me

I am autistic.
But I am only a bit autistic.
I absolutely love Lego sets.
I have this toy called a Bitzee.
And it's all about pets.

My favourite subjects are addition and division.
I like to watch Captain Underpants on television.
I like Squishmallows too.
I also like ghosts who go, "Boo!"

My favourite colour is bright, bright green.
I do not keep my room very clean.
I have a lot of Plushies.
I really like Slushies!

Jaya Pall (9)
Knockmore Primary School, Lisburn

All About Me

My name is Jared and I am very kind.
It is good to be kind I always find.
Mummy says I am very smart.
She also says I have a big heart.
Daddy says I am very funny.
My favourite food is Shreddies with honey.
I love to play basketball,
I hope I grow up to be very tall.
Pizza is my favourite tea.
This poem has been all about me.

Jared Corbett (8)
Knockmore Primary School, Lisburn

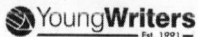

All Me

J   o is my name.
O nly child in my family.

F   riendly, fun and funny.
E veryone is my friend.
R eally good at maths.
G reat at tennis.
U nstoppable at kindness.
S ing when I'm happy.
O nly one me, I'm special.
N ever give up.

Jo Ferguson (8)
Knockmore Primary School, Lisburn

My Bestie

S he is a very kind friend

A lways being easy to find

R eally happy every day

A nd always one little call away - *Hoorah!*

Summer Hines-Pugh (9)
Knockmore Primary School, Lisburn

This Is Me

I am a picky eater,
Chocolate eater.
Pizza lover,
I love my mother.
I'm as fast as a cheetah,
And a heavy sleeper.
Football supporter,
I'm short like my mother.
Gymnastics is my favourite thing,
I like to clean but hate to sing.
When autumn is around,
I like to spin around.
I'm tiny but smart
With blue eyes, black hair
And friends who care.

Kyla Grainger (10)
Knocknagor Primary School, Trillick

This Is Me

T he sky is as blue as my eyes

H earing birds chirping makes me smile

I have brown hair

S piderman is my favourite Marvel character.

I love FIFA and football

S unny Spain is my favourite place to go.

M y favourite book is Diary of A Wimpy Kid

E very day wanting to play football.

Oisín Keenan (10)

Knocknagor Primary School, Trillick

This Is Me

T he roar of an engine makes me happy
H appy to see my friends every day
I love to work with my dad
S uper at fixing things

I love farming
S tarting to try new things

M y hobbies are working with my hands
E verything engines is my thing.

Finn Maguire (10)
Knocknagor Primary School, Trillick

This Is Me

T here are many different things about me.

H appy is a word to describe me.

I like drawing.

S ummer is my favourite season.

I like Yoshi.

S uper Mario is what I like to play.

M y mummy, she is the best.

E very day, I like to play.

Ronan McCaffrey (9)

Knocknagor Primary School, Trillick

My Symphony Of Traits

In a world of vibrant colours, I stand,
A kind and confident soul, a bit grand.
Weird yet funny, my spirits free,
A bookworm, a writer, yeah, that's me.

In the library's embrace, I find peace,
Pages whisper secrets, stories never cease.
My mind is a canvas, words my brush,
Writing stories that make hearts rush.

But don't mistake my love for the ink,
For I am a sporty soul, not one to shrink.
On fields or pitches, I find my stride,
With every victory (or loss) my passion can't hide.

Yet there's a side, a shadow deep,
Sometimes the anger in my heart does seep.
The happiness in my mind begins to leak,
The anger clogs my mind which makes me
feel weak.

In this world I'm popular, it's true,
People look up, they see what I can do.

Inspiration they find in my unique blend,
Of kindness, confidence, a loyal friend.

So here's to the kind and the funny,
To being weird, confident and sunny.
A bookworm's wisdom, a writer's pen,
A sporty heart, a popular blend.

In this life's grand tapestry, we weave,
I stand tall in my own way, believe.
A symphony of traits, a harmonious song,
Being myself where I truly belong.

Guyatu Abdullahi (10)
Lever Edge Primary Academy, Bolton

My Hopes And Me

M y family is special just like me!

Y ears passed and I have a sister and cousins too!

H opes for the future, let me see...

O ver the moon if I help stop deforestation,

P eople won't fight or anything like that,

E quality is just for me,

S adly, some of my hopes won't come true but I hope they will.

A nimals are amazing,

N early as great as me!

D iego and Bruno are the best and they love walks.

M y life is fun just like this,

E ven though nobody can stop me from being me!

Poppy Lloyd (11)
Newton Primary School, Newton

A Recipe For Ava

Cake, chocolate bar, brownie, Easter
egg rabbit, banana...
As gentle as a fluffy pet
As noisy as a loud noisy person
A litre of water
Four eggs
A litre of jelly
Chocolate, milk, Curly Wurly
Playing in the garden
Chicken, ice cream
Add a pinch of dog food
Pour in the friendly friendship
Running and playing on go-karts
Eating chocolate
First, gather books and make spaghetti
Stir in the dough
Season with love
Add some slices of cheese pizza
Then warm gently a hot chocolate
Blend the apple, pear, banana and carrot.

Jake Billingsley (8)
Newton Primary School, Newton

My Hero

Full of light, joy
Humbling and kind,
Sadness and sorrow,
Creative and clever.

A person full of happiness,
Yet anxious and stressed,
Skin and bones,
Human and imperfect.

A lion, brave and strong,
Yet devastated and pressured,
Keen and eager,
Withdrawn.

Honest and joyful,
Daring and tough,
Heartbroken,
Patient and true to herself.

Active and outgoing,
A leader,
Inspiring.

She is my hero,
And I want to be her...
A hero.

Jess Giles (10)
Newton Primary School, Newton

Free Me

I like to draw
While my dog gnaws.
I love to play with my friends every day,
Also, feed my auntie's horses some hay.
Some might play on phones or TV
But others might be interested in a simple bee.
I'm very cheeky
And sometimes sneaky.
I love to have fun
And to have hugs from my mum.
I like to relax
And learn about the Pokémon Snorlax.
I love pizza
But not the ride Rita.
Singing and dancing might fill you with glee
But me, all I want is to be free!
This is me!

Isabelle Emm (10)
Newton Primary School, Newton

My Birthday

The 25th of October,
My favourite day.
I feel sorry for those with a Christmas
birthday I must say.
Soon I will be eleven
And I will feel like heaven.
The presents are my favourite part
And it's only just the start.
I wake up at six
While everyone is in a mix.
I've been waiting for a year,
And now it's finally here.
We're going to a place with virtual reality,
And I'm struggling to keep my sanity.
Today is all about me,
Everyone will see.

Oliver Dodd (10)
Newton Primary School, Newton

This Is The Only Me

I am a person who puts anything to mind.
My sporty personality is some sporty fun.
My funny bro could drive things crazy.
My fantastic football team is willing to score goals.
My favourite holiday is tasting Spanish Fever.
My best friend is making things funny.
My amazing school makes learning fun.
My favourite footballer, scoring for LFC.
My favourite football club is right across
the Mersey.
My brain, no shame, it's just an amazing
superpower.
This is the only me.

Zach Kennah (10)
Newton Primary School, Newton

All About Me

First, gather my pets, lots of cuddles and my
parents for snuggles,
Now, off to school, then get home, stir some cake
mix and shove in the oven,
Season in the summer, going on holiday to
Kefalonia (Greek island),
Add in a pinch of water fights to cool off the heat,
Then, pour in winter snowball fights, jackets on,
very cold and Christmas and birthday too,
Blend a smoothie, nearly the next year,
Then settle into the next year with my family,
parents and pets too.

Jake Mylchreest (8)
Newton Primary School, Newton

I'm Enough

Pen or toy
Girl or boy
Large or skinny
Serious or silly
Tall or small
You're enough the way you are
Your looks don't matter
No matter what
Race
Sex
Religion
You're amazing if you're crazy
No one is perfect
Everybody has flaws
But remember to get a good education
Because it will open many doors
And when you're feeling down
Say this to your town...
I'm enough!

Katie Spellman (10)
Newton Primary School, Newton

To Create Me

10 lb of fun and playfulness
A lot of football
3 lb of chicken nugget lover
90% sporty
A bit of kindness and generosity
Some helpfulness and usefulness
0.1111 of laziness
Sharpshooter
Fast as a cheetah
Crazy like a monkey
Messy like a pig
Funny like a clown
Friendly like a Labrador
Super like Superman
Happy like a dog
Tall like a giraffe
Serious like a tiger.

Marco Stather (11)
Newton Primary School, Newton

My Recipe For My Pet

First, I will gather eagerly and travel
And I will gather kindness, cuddles and then fun.
Then I will bake chocolate cake
Then I will wait for 15 minutes.
Add a chocolate banana
Then a chocolate rabbit.
Then for my chocolate cake, I will add frosting.
Then I'll call my cat, Cookie Moon.
Stir in kindness and walkies and cuddles then life.
Season with fun, kindness and eating puddings.

Scarlett Lennon (8)
Newton Primary School, Newton

This Is Me

First, gather football and generosity.
Second, stir in love, cuddles, kisses and games.
Third, season with pudding, parties and
adventures.
Fourth, add a pinch of art and sleep.
Fifth, pour in a world worth of trust.
Then a bit of my mum's chocolate cake
and kindness.
Blend in a lot of noise and lots of amazing
surprises.
Then warm gentle hugs.
Then a good friend and family member.

Naya Elmenshawy (8)
Newton Primary School, Newton

The Wood Wanderer

My fur is the colour of autumn leaves
I have a fluffy tail like a feather duster.
My nose is like a button and I have eyes like
marbles.
My teeth are like dominos
And I have needle-like nails.

I nibble nuts all day long.
I climb and climb until I reach the sun.
I have so much energy I jump like a ball
And I annoy almost all.
I run about from tree to tree.
Can you guess me?

Kate Giles (10)
Newton Primary School, Newton

Kenzi's Secret K3 Recipe

First, gather craziness and cuteness,
Stir in a world full of Kallie's teddies,
Add a season of playfights with Daddy,
Put in a pinch of silliness,
Pour in an ocean's worth of love,
Sprinkle loads of adventures with Grandad,
Blend in some sniffs and licks,
Then warm gently by having snuggles and
cuddles with my family,
Finally, top it off with some squirrels.

Kallie Vincent (8)
Newton Primary School, Newton

A Recipe For My Brother, Scott

First, gather intelligence and interesting reading.
Stir in an ocean of chocolate or yummy food.
Season with a bed of sleeping and lots of tennis.
Add a pinch of unharmful play fighting and messing around.
Pour in an enormous tablespoon of adventure and running.
Blend with naughtiness and laughter, ice cream and climbing.
Then warm gently with lots of trust and loving colours.

Rowan Cornwell (8)
Newton Primary School, Newton

This Is Me

Football's my sport
Though I don't mind being on a tennis court.
Dylan's my name
And sport is my game.

I love my cat
But love to chillax!
I'm really funny
And always love it when it's sunny.

In football, I'm a creator,
But I also love being a baker.
I am really kind
And I will take anything in my stride.

Dylan Shaw (10)
Newton Primary School, Newton

How To Create Me

A sharpshooter
Fast as the Flash
Food lover
95% sporty
Crazy as a monkey
Super like Superman
Helpful as a horse
Friendly like a fish
10000 lb of football
10000 lb of fun and playfulness
Noisy like an elephant
10 lb of pizza
Funny as a clown
Rough as a tiger
Strong as a rhino
Tough as a hippo
Small as a squirrel.

Freddy Armstrong (10)
Newton Primary School, Newton

This Is Me

T idying books only to mess them up again

H aving a younger brother is such a pain in the head.

I n the night, the stars are so cool but...

S inging in the shower is another story to unfold.

I ntelligence is key but I'm

S inging like a freak.

M emories are everything.

E ither way, I love me.

Sumaiya Khan (10)
Newton Primary School, Newton

A Poem For A Kitten Called Coco

First, gather your favourite toys and
favourite balls.
Stir in all of her favourite toys in a big tub,
Season with cuddles and kisses,
Add a pinch of knowing that you are not
going to hurt her,
Pour in a wide handful of trust and kindness
that she deserves every day,
Blend games and toys,
Then warm gently by having cuddles and
meaning it.

Lucy Hodson (8)
Newton Primary School, Newton

How To Make A Good Atherton Racer

First, gather determination and skill,
Stir in a pinch of races and World Cup wins,
Season with forty successes,
Add a pinch of a great mum,
Pour in some fantastic wheels and bikes,
May have retired, but still going well,
Blend in some Endura and bell,
Then warm gently by shredding the track,
And the fastest mum on two wheels is
coming back.

Idris Thomas (9)
Newton Primary School, Newton

This Is All About My Puppy

All about love and kindness
My puppy is a tan colour
And a pinch of love and naughtiness for my dog
He is a month old and he likes to chew toys
and bones
And his favourite toy is shoes
He likes to dig up my back garden
He is very naughty
He likes my sister's toes and my ankles
So when he is in the room we have to put
on shoes!

Aiyla Stamp (8)
Newton Primary School, Newton

Secret Animal

This animal is a spiky fur ball.
It is very cute and very small.
It is certainly the best but it doesn't build a nest.
It eats slugs and snails and I'm glad it can't
eat whales.
It sleeps in the day and is awake at night.
And if you sit on it, it will give you a very big fright.
What could my secret animal be?

Scott Cornwell (11)
Newton Primary School, Newton

A Recipe For Dad

First, gather a screwdriver and a white van.
Stir in games and cuddles.
Season with friends and help.
Add a pinch of family and blue eyes.
Pour in white and blue colours.
And always laughing, smiling and happy.
Blend kindness and surprise with adventures
and enjoyment.
Then warm gently with happiness and enjoyment.

Poppy-Ella Coathup Pinches (8)

Newton Primary School, Newton

Me

Wrexham
Overcome fears
Wales... Yma o Hyd!
F1, Lando Norris.
Comes down the straight to fans galore.
Lewis Hamilton,
Already at the end,
Oh look, he's won again.
Rugby, in the pack,
Twickenham, in the stack.
Alan Wyn Jones and Louis Rees Zammit,
Kicking it to the summit.

This is me!

Jacob Heap (10)
Newton Primary School, Newton

This Is My Cat, Poppy

First, gather bravery and cuteness.
Next, stir in an ocean of mice.
Season with tickles and adventures.
Add a pinch of destroying birds.
Pour in a pinch of cuddles
And a tiny bit of funniness and more cuddles.
Blend cuddles, cuddles and more cuddles.
Then warm gently by calling Poppy and
cuddling her forever.

Elliot Shaw (8)
Newton Primary School, Newton

A Recipe For A Mouse Named Star

First, gather boldness and quick-wittedness,
Stir in a bowl of favourite food,
Season with a sprinkle of mealworms,
Add a pinch of patience,
Pour in an armful of fun,
And an evening of play and games,
Blend scurries and sniffs, snuggles and nibbles,
Then warm gently by saying,
She really is a super Star!

Alice Crimp (9)
Newton Primary School, Newton

Recipe For A Life

First, gather cuddles and love.
Stir in a tub of lovely friendliness.
Season with long adventures and family laughs.
Add a pinch of lying down and tickles with us.
And have lots of fun between us.
Blend in dreams and games with cuddles
and tickles
Finally, warm gently by lying down and
calming strokes.

Josh Barlow Ashworth (8)
Newton Primary School, Newton

My Dog, Duke

First, gather sleeping and snoring,
Stir in a tub of balls to chew,
Season with games of eating and running,
Add a pinch of copying your brother to get a treat,
Pour in a teardrop when you're feeling lonely,
Add a drop of wags and strokes, kisses and misses,
Then warm gently by their heart-warming
happiness.

Zara Ates (8)
Newton Primary School, Newton

Me

My name is Lope
I am...
A black ten-year-old
Who does not clean his room
I am really energetic maybe even dumb
But I know one thing for sure,
I really love my mum.
My mum is sometimes sad
And that doesn't make me glad.
She is really kind and nice
And I want to make her happy.

Oluwalolope Femi-Pius (10)
Newton Primary School, Newton

My Recipe Poem For My Cat

First, I will get some eggs and flowers
And mix it all, then make a bone shape
Then put in the oven for 15 minutes.
Take it out, get some frosting
And write my cat's names on the cookie moon.
Then put it in the fridge for the night
Then take it out and you can give it to your cat
or dog.

Imani Uddin (8)
Newton Primary School, Newton

A Recipe For My Dog

I gather treats and toys.
Stir in lots of tummy tickles.
Season with games of adventures.
Add a pinch of naughtiness.
Pour in some barking
And jumping up at each other.
Blend in the licking, cuddles and loveliness
Then warm gently by saying 'dindins' and
meaning it.

Poppy Tromans (8)
Newton Primary School, Newton

A Recipe For My Sister

First, gather a sweet, loving person,
With a nice smile,
Stir in lots of cuddles,
A hot chocolate and some love,
Pour in honesty, loyalty and trust in me,
Add some love so you know I love you so,
Shine some sun because you are bright as a star,
You shine bright like a diamond.

Sameena Uddin (8)
Newton Primary School, Newton

Recipe Of My Little Dog

First, gather cuddles and snuggles,
Stir in smelly toys,
Season with chasing cats,
Add a pinch of love and care,
Pour in kisses and likes,
And repeat your loving heart.

Blend hearts and kisses,
Then warm gently by cuddling up in bed
and having long, lovely walks.

Dahlia Walsh (8)
Newton Primary School, Newton

A Recipe For My Kitten

First, gather toys and a bed.
Stir in some cuddles and tickles.
Season with some food.
Add a pinch of craziness.
Pour in water and dry food.
Add only colourful ones.
Blend socks and adventures with kindness
and surprises.
Then warm gently by having fun with her family.

James Hodson
Newton Primary School, Newton

This Is Me

I'm a star in the night, shining bright
A son climbing with his mum
I'm a child who plays the guitar
And even does lessons for fun
I'm a kid who loves playing football
with my friends too
If you're my friend then you'll certainly
know what position I do.

Arthur March (10)
Newton Primary School, Newton

My Hero Wilbur

First, gather all his favourite toys,
Then stir in a pond of mud,
Seasons of mud stinking and drying off,
Add some wild barks,
Pour in the toys!
And daftness,
Blend sniffs and snuggles, licks and cuddles,
Then, warm gently by saying 'walkies' and
meaning it.

Ben Cooper (9)
Newton Primary School, Newton

My Hamster, Fierce

First, gather fun and cuteness.
Stir in a tub of food.
Season with games of climbing.
Add a pinch of sleeping.
Pour in some nosiness.
And a little cute nose.
Blend adventurousness with playing
And cuddling with a funny nose.
Then warm gently by adding playfulness.

Molly Lee (8)
Newton Primary School, Newton

My Dog

My pet is gentle and fun.
I like to see her playing.
First, gather a chew toy and a dog.
Stir in a chew toy.
Season with dogs.
Pour in dogs and more dogs.
Blend in dogs and dogs and dogs!
Then warm with gentle hugs.
She is always there when I need her.

Ethan Powell (8)
Newton Primary School, Newton

For All My Family

First, gather love and wonder,
Stir in a loving bowl,
Season with dads and mums,
Add a pinch of brothers and sisters,
Pour in hugs and love,
And laughs and naps,
Blend love and puffs,
Then warm gently by roaring love
For everyone and stay the same.

James Shennan (8)
Newton Primary School, Newton

Licks And Cuddles

First, gather energy and lots of treats,
Stir in a lot of cuteness and fun,
Season with a game of fetch,
Add a pinch of taste while you pant,
Pour in an earth full of trust,
And gets what he wants every day,
Blends in with cuddles,
Then barks in glory.

Rosemae Armstrong (8)
Newton Primary School, Newton

My Mother

I don't listen to others
I love my mother
She helps me see
What I truly can be
She boosts my self-esteem
She helps me let off my steam
She cares for me
She loves tea
She's the trunk of my tree
This is me...
This is me...

Jos Hearse (10)
Newton Primary School, Newton

My Very Own Recipe

First, gather some delicious chocolate treats
And then season with some things about you
like fun and silliness.
Second, sprinkle things you like like parties
and games.
Third, gather some blackberries and strawberries.
Finally, warm it by cooking.

Daniel Georgiev (8)
Newton Primary School, Newton

My Rabbit

First, gather 'gives lots of hugs'.
Stir in 'buy lots of food'.
Add a pinch of 'gets lots of toys'.
Season with 'jumps like he's on a pogo stick'.
Pour in 'love to jump'.
Blend with 'he is super fast'.

Benjamin Foxton (8)
Newton Primary School, Newton

Me

Small but strong
And a very good helper
Good at PE but a very bad speller
This is me
I like to play football
And I support the best team
LFC is the name
This is me
Good at running
Good at rugby
Bad at dancing
This is me!

Saif Uddin

Newton Primary School, Newton

My Sister

First, gather chocolate buttons and
chocolate cake.
Stir in Peppa Pig and Cocomelon.
Season with sweet animals.
Add a pinch of eating pudding.
Pour in toys and cuddles.
Blend with parties, games and silliness.
Then warm by giving cuddles.

Lily Otton (8)
Newton Primary School, Newton

My Sister's Success

First, gather fun and make-up
Stir in a tub of baking
Season with imaginative adventures
Add a pinch of games
Pour in a world of love
And that never-ending laughter
Blend in sweets and beats
Then warm gently with a hot cup of tea.

Orla Lloyd (8)
Newton Primary School, Newton

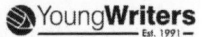

This Is My Animal

They are big furry creatures.
Sometimes they have tough tusks.
In the forests of Europe, they lurk.
But are hunted for fun.
They can end up on your dinner plate.
This is my animal.
What is it?

Answer: Wild boar.

Alexander Robertshaw-Lewis (10)
Newton Primary School, Newton

Willow

First, get a bell and a mirror.
Stir in flappy wings.
Season with little feathers.
Add a pinch of green and blue.
Pair in sitting on shoulders.
Add living in a cage.
Blend in taking a bath.
Then eat seed and drink water.

Jennifer-Rose Thompson (8)
Newton Primary School, Newton

This Is Me

Fast runner
Scary jumper
Loud singer
Funny actor
Quick dancer
Calm reader
Hungry eater
Family hugger
Graceful swimmer
Peacemaker
Art creator
History lover
English writer

This is me!

Francesca Mylchreest (10)
Newton Primary School, Newton

This Is Me

First, gather and relax.
Stir in lots of cats.
Season with games of Fortnite.
Add a pinch of tickles from anyone.
And positiveness for everything.
Blend puddings and kindness.
Then warm gently with books of quiet reading.

George Dodd (8)
Newton Primary School, Newton

Recipe For My Dad

First, gather being brave and sporty,
Stir in a tub of lovingness,
Season with wise cooking,
Pour in trusting him,
And knowing he lets me buy stuff,
Blend making him laugh,
Then warm gently by giving hugs and kisses.

Pippa Jackson (8)
Newton Primary School, Newton

What Am I?

I'm as fluffy as a dog
But I'm as vicious as a tiger.
I come out at night,
I'm a really good climber.
I can swim, jump, scratch,
My favourite food is fish.
What am I?

Answer: A bear.

Alfred Evans-Wood (10)
Newton Primary School, Newton

A Recipe For Iola

First, gather lots of love,
Stir in a teddy bear,
Season with cheeky grins,
Add a pinch of fun and games,
Pour in some adventures,
And hearts that care,
Blend stories,
Then warm gently with lots of cuddles.

Cerys Malone (9)
Newton Primary School, Newton

Recipe Of My Cat, Oreo

First, gather trust and happiness,
Stir in a tub of tunnels and treats,
Season with games of 'Catch the Mouse',
And make sure we try new things,
Blend tickling and snuggling,
Then come closer and buy the trust.

Evie Docking (9)
Newton Primary School, Newton

How To Make Wilson The Dog

Add 3.5 per cent black fur and a pinch of white.
Let it cook and add a lot of goofiness and cheekiness.
Then mix funniness and happiness to make joy.
Add it in.
Once you hear a bowl smash, your Wilson has arrived!

Edward Boyce (10)

Newton Primary School, Newton

Recipe For Myself

A chunk of love.
A dash of kindness.
A sprinkle of life.
An ounce of books.
A pinch of gymnastics.
A drop of friends.
A dribble of besties.
An eye for food.
A pint of animals.
This is me.

Elizabeth Wall (10)
Newton Primary School, Newton

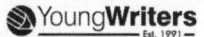

Recipe Of My Sister, Juni

First, gather happiness and creativity.
Stir in Lego games and season with playing
in the garden.
Pour in an ocean's worth of hope and cuddles
and funniness and joy.
Then warm the love of being a sister.

Frank Ivory (8)
Newton Primary School, Newton

Life

Life, what a wonderful thing.
Think of all that it brings.
You should embrace it for all that it brings.
Its wrongs, its rights, its mistakes and its
ups and downs
For this is life and it only comes once.

Martha Storey (10)
Newton Primary School, Newton

Recipe Of Me

First, gather some happiness and calm down
Season with some joy
Stir in some excitement and add a pinch of silliness
Pour in a tub of cuteness
Then blend it with some sweetness
Then you get warm cuddles.

Zimal Baiq (8)
Newton Primary School, Newton

This Is Me

Animal lover
Amazing dancer
Awesome drawer
Brilliant baker
Family hugger
Loud singer
Loyal leaper
Graceful swimmer
English writer
Calm reader
Smart actor
Peacemaker.

Aoibheann Gunessee (10)

Newton Primary School, Newton

Recipe For My Mum

First, gather cuddles and bedtime stories,
Stir in kindness,
Season with playing,
Add a pinch of smiles,
Pour in fun and new things every day,
Blend walks,
Then warm by healing hurt things.

Jacob Lewis (8)
Newton Primary School, Newton

My Name Is Daisy

My name is Daisy,
I'm a bit crazy,
I love jumping on people,
Especially when we score in football.
I love being crazy,
And playing all day.
I love snails too,
Wahoo,
Yay!

Daisy Roberts (10)
Newton Primary School, Newton

Lazy Liyana

My name's Liyana
And they call me Lazy Liyana.
And I love to eat food.
If you mess with me I'll kick you.
I have many friends but forget them.
I'm too cool for school!

Liyana Haque (10)
Newton Primary School, Newton

This Is Who I Am

B asketball warrior.

E nergetic creature.

L ovely friend.

L uscious dogs.

A nnoying talker.

Bella Brown (11)

Newton Primary School, Newton

Me

I am a...

J oyful friend
U nderstanding
N aughty mischief maker
I am me.

Juni Ivory (10)
Newton Primary School, Newton

Hank

H appy forever
A mazing forever
N oisy forever
K ind forever!

Hank Starck (10)

Newton Primary School, Newton

This Is Me

My name is Ida and I'm in Year Five
My mother tells me she's full of pride
Rain or shine, the theatre is always mine
Happiness comes in lots of places
Forever filling all the spaces
My brother, Oliver, makes me laugh
Always picking the silly path
Reading and writing are my friends
Building friendships that will never end
Thank you for listening to my poem
All about myself, I'm constantly growing.

Ida Ainsworth-Ballinger (9)

North Lancing Primary School, Lancing

A Recipe That Just Makes Me

My name is Josh, I'm nearly eight,
I'm always up early,
I'm never late,
People always tell me that I am quite tall,
But starting a new school, I feel so small.
I have left Church Gresley and started at Pennine,
Mum walks me to school and tells me I'll be fine.
The school is so much bigger than my last,
But I like it a lot and the days go fast.
I'm always polite in everything I do,
I never forget to say "please" and "thank you".
I'm sometimes quiet, I'm sometimes loud,
My mum always says I make her proud.
I enjoy playing Roblox and football too,
My favourite colour in the world is blue,
Pizza is my favourite food to eat,
Followed by ice cream is a real treat.
This is a poem of a recipe of me,
I always try to be the best I can be.

Joshua Bell (7)
Pennine Way Junior Academy, Swadlincote

Be Myself

Being myself is what I do,
Being someone else is not being you.

I get inspired but don't repeat,
I make lots of meals that you can eat.

I'll make an outfit by hand that is neat,
But I won't make you wear it if you don't like it.

I can be wacky and wild, so don't always fit in,
But I still have lots of friends who will listen.

Sometimes I can be a bit of a nerd,
That doesn't mean I can't be a part of the herd.

Sharing and caring is what I do,
So I try my hardest not to be blue.

Being blue will upset your moods,
So let's try to be happy and sing a song.

Because...
We are all unique,
So I just have to be me,
And don't you dare copy a word.

Grace Vorley (10)
Pennine Way Junior Academy, Swadlincote

I Am Made Of Colour

Red is when I'm angry, usually with my brother.
Orange is when I'm excited about holidays and seeing friends.
Yellow is when I'm happy being with my friends and having fun.
Green is when I'm scared of spiders and strange places at night; they give me a fright.
Blue is when I'm sad. Being sad is not nice but cuddles and snuggles make it better.
Pink is when I'm loving, giving cuddles and smiles.
Purple is when I'm asleep; Mum and Dad think this is the best time.
Then, sprinkle me with magic dust because I'm just a little bit magic and special.

Martha Topley (8)

Pennine Way Junior Academy, Swadlincote

What Makes Me Unique

C is for cheesy pasta, my favourite food.

A is for art, I like to draw.

R is for riding around on my bike.

I is for iPad, I love to play games.

N is for numbers.

G is for being a good friend.

K is for keen, I'm eager to learn.

I is for imagination, I like to make up stories.

N is for nighttime when I like to read my books.

D is for dancing all night long when I like to sing my favourite song.

Clara McGill (7)

Pennine Way Junior Academy, Swadlincote

This Is Me

This is me
Take a look at what you see
I'm amazing, happy and fun
And I like to throw in the odd pun
I like to read books
So pop into your library and have a look
You'll find me in there
But remember not to stare
I like long and short walks
But I am known to talk!
One of my talents is art
Which comes from the heart
This is me
Take a look at what you see
I'm amazing, happy and fun
And I like to throw in the odd pun.

Faith Smith (9)

Pennine Way Junior Academy, Swadlincote

The Girl You'll Meet

Teal is my favourite colour like the vibrant sea,
Kindness and caring, that's how I like to be.
With ginger hair that dances like flames,
Hazel-coloured eyes, where adventure claims.
I wear glasses, you see, a part of my style,
They make me unique and they make me smile.
I dance with joy, my feet in a groove
Sensitive but positive that's how I move.
So here's my little poem, simple and sweet,
About the things I love, the girl you'll meet.

Billie-Rae Mack (8)

Pennine Way Junior Academy, Swadlincote

All About Me

This is all about me.

When things don't go my way
I'll usually forget
And go out 'n' play.

This is all about me.

My favourite place is where you get a book,
a vacation for your mind
Go and see, you'll be amazed, go take a look.

This is all about me.

Now that I'm nearly done, goodbye!
Until next time...
Thank the lord from the sky.

Lily-Rose Evans (8)
Pennine Way Junior Academy, Swadlincote

All About Me

My name is Lilia
I'm so crazy
I like to eat sweets
But I'm a bit lazy

I'm a very sweet girl
I love to sing
My favourite colour is pastel pink
And maths is my thing

I have lots of pets
I love them all
Bunnies are my favourite
I love to play with my dog and her ball.

Lilia Ruston (9)
Pennine Way Junior Academy, Swadlincote

Beach Day!

Yesterday
I went to the sea
And I saw a palm tree
It was green
Clean and humongous.

Then I chilled
On the sand
While listening to
My favourite band.

It was very cool
Thinking about jewels
So, I got up to search for pearls
With some of my girls.

Danielle Sharp (10)
Pennine Way Junior Academy, Swadlincote

I Am Special!

A bbie is my name
B rave is what I am
B e kind is my motto
I always love to dance
E veryone knows I love nature

J ust you wait and see
O nce you get to know me, you will know I am very friendly.

Abbie-Jo Collier (8)
Pennine Way Junior Academy, Swadlincote

I Love Food

I love food, oh yes I do
I would eat any food (except mushrooms)
Think of anything you could name
I wouldn't ever play a game
Bingy, bongy, bongy, ba
Hip, hip hooray
Oh, just think of any food you could name
Hip hip hooray.

Ryan Inight (8)
Pennine Way Junior Academy, Swadlincote

Untitled

I am cool
I am cute
I am beautiful

My friend is Ella
My friend is Savana
My friend is Mia

My favourite colour is red
My favourite colour is blue
My favourite colour is yellow.

Laciee Mitchener (7)
Pennine Way Junior Academy, Swadlincote

Happy To Be Me

Blonde is my hair colour.
Blue are my eyes.
I'm seven years old.
And just the right size.
My name is Amelia,
And, as you can see,
I'm very happy
To be *me*!

Amelia Dyke (7)
Pennine Way Junior Academy, Swadlincote

Sparkling Gymnasts

On the bars, I can reach the stars.
It is so very high I feel like I might fly.

On the beam, I feel like I am a queen.
Elegantly, I point my toes and take a step
and make a pose.

On the floor, I can impress,
With a cartwheel or round-off and arabesque.

Next is the vault where I jump and somersault.

Last is a trampette where I bounce really high to
Reach the sky.

Now the competition is over, I wait till I'm told,
I won gold!

Amelie Wong (8)
Rockmount Primary School, Upper Norwood

I Am

I like the colour of the violet tulips and the bright blue sky.
Cheetahs are my favourite animal.
I love Christmas because of spending time with my family.
I am the wind and the breeze.
I like the colour of violet tulips and the bright blue sky.
I love the sound of kittens playing because this is me.
I am the wind and the breeze, this is me.

Audrey Neil (7)
Rockmount Primary School, Upper Norwood

Me

A heap of kindness
A pinch of anger
A sprinkle of fidgeting
A cup of happiness
A mountain of craziness
A handful of blisters
50g of boredom
A truck full of tickle hatred
A bed full of sleeping
That is me!

Amber Bartle (7)
Rockmount Primary School, Upper Norwood

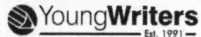

I Am Gabriel

I am a friend and kind.
I wonder why the moon is white and the sky is blue.
I hear the car beeping and the TV playing.
I see the waves bashing and foxes.
I want a Nintendo Switch and roller skates.
I am friendly and joyful.

Gabriel Shapcott (8)

Rockmount Primary School, Upper Norwood

What I Am

I am cute and dangerous
I wonder why penguins cannot fly
I hear birds tweeting outside
I see paradise like it's waiting for me
I want a Nintendo and a dog
I am cute and dangerous.

Amir Douglas (7)
Rockmount Primary School, Upper Norwood

The Black Mamba Strike

I am a golden, Black Mamba.
I wonder if my species are in danger!
I hear other snakes slithering around me.
I see an army of snakes.
I want to strike.

Miles E Peters (7)
Rockmount Primary School, Upper Norwood

All About Me

Strictly and purple are two of my favourite things!
I also like pandas and I love to sing!
I like to draw and I like to run, run!
Being me is very fun!

Frank Wilson (7)

Rockmount Primary School, Upper Norwood

This Is Me

I am kind, confident, supportive
And I am good at drama.
Because helping people
I support my friends,
I wonder if I will ever get fans.

I worry that I won't get better
At maths - it is so annoying.

I dream that everyone
Will want my autograph
And I am a star.

I try to get the
Main parts in the plays.

I want to have lots of dresses
And lots of chocolate.

I fear that my mum
Is overdoing things.

I love my family and my friends
Because they are always
There for me.

This is beautiful.

Lauren Galloway-Doherty (10)
Sion Mills Primary School, Sion Mills

This Is Me

I am a gamer, I love playing video games, it's
my favourite thing to do.
I wonder if I am going to have a good birthday.
I worry when I fly in a plane because I don't like it.
I dream I can start playing football.
I try my best at school work and homework
independently.
I want to ride my bike more.
I fear spiders, they look scary, and I don't
like them.
I love Earth because it has everything on it.

Riley McNamee (11)
Sion Mills Primary School, Sion Mills

This Is Me

I am... a footballer.

I wonder... how Ronaldo can jump so high?

I worry... about my grandad and granny.

I dream... to play on a professional football pitch whilst playing with Manchester United.

I try... my best at football matches and training.

I want... to win the Champions League with Man United and win the Euros or the World Cup with Ireland.

I fear... not becoming a footballer.

I love... football.

Tom Hyndman
Sion Mills Primary School, Sion Mills

This Is Me!

I am a good Gaelic football player.
I wonder what will happen when I am older and
if I will like being an adult.
I worry about what people think of me, especially
my friends.
I dream about owning a real-life panda!
I try to help everyone and not leave anyone out.
I want to stop climate change and people smoking
and vaping.
I fear big spiders.
I love my family.

Aoife Kelly (10)
Sion Mills Primary School, Sion Mills

This Is Me!

I am kind and very respectful.
I wonder if my grandads' are okay now.
I worry about my brother getting hurt
because I love him.
I dream that when I grow up I still love art.
I try to get my brother to help clean our room.
I want to get better at art and reading.
I fear slugs! They are slimy and disgusting.
I love bunnies, art and my friends and family.

Mia Bradley (10)
Sion Mills Primary School, Sion Mills

This Is Me

I am a farmer, an animal lover,
And someone who talks a lot.
I wonder, will I buy a boat when I'm older?
I worry if my dog gets hit by a car,
Because I love her.
I dream of being a dairy farmer.
I try my best to get better
At football and basketball.
I want to have more farm cats.
I fear more farm cats dying.
I love dogs, cats and my family.

Ollie Millar
Sion Mills Primary School, Sion Mills

This Is Me

I am a footballer who loves animals
I wonder if I will like high school
I worry about my great-granny
I dream about becoming a professional
football player
I try to be better at goalkeeping in football
I want tickets to see Manchester United play
I fear spiders, seeing spiders makes me tingly
I love animals, football and seeing Manchester
United play.

Alex Patterson (10)
Sion Mills Primary School, Sion Mills

This Is Me

I am the kindest person in the class.
I am a gamer, I love playing video games.
I wonder how deep the ocean is.
I wonder how far space is.
I worry about people being sad.

I dream about being a swimmer.
I try to be better at my times tables.
I want a set of Boomwhackers.
I fear wasps because I got stung one time.
I love my mummy and daddy.

Lincoln Harpur (10)
Sion Mills Primary School, Sion Mills

This Is Me

I am... a good, trustworthy friend who is kind.
I wonder... why people are mean.
I worry... about the change I will have to go
through post-primary.
I dream... of being famous.
I try... to always do my best.
I want... to make my family proud.
I fear... snakes because they freak me out.
I love... my family.
This is me! This is me! This is me!

Maya Catterson (10)
Sion Mills Primary School, Sion Mills

This Is Me

I am a Gaelic player for Urnaí
I wonder if will we beat Naomb
Eoghan at the next under-twelves match
I worry about my cat getting stuck up
a tree again for the fifth time
I dream of playing Gaelic for Tyrone or Donegal
I try to get all my work done
I want to beat Naomb Eoghan next year
I fear spiders or any type of bug
I love my family.

Holly Moore (10)
Sion Mills Primary School, Sion Mills

This Is Me

I am smart, kind, happy, beautiful, enthusiastic
and brave.
I wonder why a lot
I worry about my granny,
I dream of swimming with sharks and getting
a dog,
I try to do cartwheels,
I want so many things,
Last but not least, I want to get better at
cartwheels.
I fear bats but I also think they are cute.
I love my family and friends.

Jayne Annesley
Sion Mills Primary School, Sion Mills

This Is Me!

I am... intelligent, unique, calm, simple.
I wonder... why I am so short?
I worry... that my flight to Manchester will be cancelled.
I dream... about being a professional football player.
I try... to be the best I can be!
I want... to get better at football.
I fear... not finishing my homework on time.
I love... everyone in my family.

Oliver Williamson (10)
Sion Mills Primary School, Sion Mills

This Is Me...

I am a short, funny human being.
I wonder what it would be like to be a
professional footballer.
I worry about my nannie and granda.
I dream about being a professional footballer.
I try to do my best in everything.
I want my great-grandmother back from heaven.
I fear losing my family.
I love spending time with my grandparents.

Cara Brown (10)
Sion Mills Primary School, Sion Mills

This Is Me

I am a loyal and kind friend to all.
I wonder who made God.
I worry that I am not ready for post-primary.
I dream that I get my dream job
And a happy family.
I try my best in everything I do.
I want world happiness
And all schools integrated.
I fear not being able to play football.
I love everything in my life.

Farrah Crompton-Pattison (10)
Sion Mills Primary School, Sion Mills

This Is Me

I am joyful, kind and a good listener
I wonder what I am going to do when I get home
I worry about getting something wrong
I dream that I will be good at school
I try to be good at school
I want my dad to live right next door to me
I fear spiders because their legs look scary
I love my family.

Kamile Elijosiute (11)
Sion Mills Primary School, Sion Mills

This Is Me

I am courageous, zealous, warm-hearted
and virtuous.
I wonder, are unicorns real?
I worry about having a child when I'm older.
I dream about winning a show jumping
competition.
I try to be kind and reliable.
I want a horse.
I fear spiders, clowns and deep water.
I love my dog, Toby.

Gracey Hamilton (10)
Sion Mills Primary School, Sion Mills

This Is Me

I am kind, caring and funny.
I wonder why my brother is crazy.
I worry my brother is plotting something.
I dream to be a professional rugby player
for Ireland.
I try to be the best I can be.
I want dogs to live forever.
I fear my brother.
I love my mum, dad and dogs and maybe brother.

Tom Freeborn
Sion Mills Primary School, Sion Mills

This Is Me

I am a dog lover and a horse lover.
I wonder when I am going to canter.
I worry about my family's health.
I dream of owning a horse yard.
I try to do all my work neat and tidy.
I want to own my own horse one day.
I fear spiders because they are scary.
I love horse riding so much.

Ellie Magee (11)
Sion Mills Primary School, Sion Mills

This Is Me

I am kind, helpful and caring.
I wonder what I am going to be when I grow up.
I worry about speaking in front of the class.
I dream about being a gymnast.
I try to be the best I can be.
I want to be able to see without my glasses.
I fear going to school.
I love my family.

Alyssia Calvert (10)
Sion Mills Primary School, Sion Mills

This Is Me

I am not perfect but I am good enough.
I wonder why we have dreams.
I worry about my little brother.
I dream that I will get a car when I am older.
I try to do my best at work.
I want the Fortnite Battle Pass.
I fear death.
I love my mum.

Keelim Moore (10)
Sion Mills Primary School, Sion Mills

This Is Me

I wonder what it's like being a family member.
I worry that I won't make it as a football player.
I dream of being a pro football player.
I try my best.
I want the best of myself.
I fear getting lost.
I love football.

Patrick Colhoun
Sion Mills Primary School, Sion Mills

This Is Me

I am smart
I wonder if there is life in space
I worry about life because life leads to death
I dream one day I might fly
I try to get better at cricket
I want the universe
I fear big needles
I love my dogs.

Harry Adams (10)
Sion Mills Primary School, Sion Mills

Baking Me

Set the oven to 20 degrees,
Nice and warm, with a slight breeze,
Mix the maths and literacy,
In a bowl with art and DT.

My life is like a recipe,
It takes a long time to bake me,
The arts and crafts, the singing and writing,
Sieve them, whisk them, but don't start fighting.

Most of the time I'm not sad, but happy,
Though my brother sometimes makes me angry,
I like to think I'm kind and helpful,
But sometimes life can get too stressful.

Put it in the oven (at 20°C),
Don't fiddle with the knobs,
Or I might freeze.

Mix all the icing,
1, 2, 3.
Now you know,
How to bake me.

Hannah Dowle (9)
Southway Primary School, Bognor Regis

This Is Me

My nickname is Fee and this is me.
I love going to school
Because learning is cool.
I love to cook
Using my mom's recipe book.
I read Harry Potter at night
With my camping light.
My nickname is Fee and this is me.
I'm really fast
I never come last.
It's time to sleep
I set my alarm clock to beep.
See you tomorrow at school,
Make sure you don't break a single rule.
My nickname is Fee and this is me.

Sofia Delieu-Gaitan (9)
Southway Primary School, Bognor Regis

I Love Halloween

I like the way it goes
You can dress up in spooky costumes
You do this every year
You might dress up as a witch or a pumpkin
Imagine there's a ghost behind you
That would be creepy now.

Once it's Christmas it's not as bad
But not like in my poem
Well, your creepy costumes or pumpkins
It goes so fast.

Anna Barthik (7)
Southway Primary School, Bognor Regis

Matthew

M ighty good friend
A lways amazing and ambitious
T otally dependable
T rustworthy and tremendously funny
H elpful and handy to have around
E nthusiastic and encouraging
W arm-hearted and wonderful.

R eliable and resilient
A wonderful listener
N ice and nature-loving
K ind and caring
I nteresting and intelligent
N ever mean, naughty or negative.

Matthew Rankin (8)
St Matthew's CE Primary School, West Wimbledon

Edward

E dward is so bright, I make people laugh day and night.

D ay and night, I do funny faces if people are feeling sad.

W onderful and helpful little boy.

A ctive and sporty is me.

R apid and speedy, I love running, it is just for me.

D ancing isn't really my thing but I love playing with my family and friends. I also like reading.

Edward Jarman (8)
St Matthew's CE Primary School, West Wimbledon

Bright

B ouncing up and down with joy.

R eally enjoying myself that's for sure.

I nventing lots of fun games, that's another definite aim!

G ames are fun and playing them is too.

H appily, I play with my bright crew.

T ogether we will have loads of fun, inventing games for everyone.

Senara Bacon (8)
St Matthew's CE Primary School, West Wimbledon

Izabella

I love to play with my friends.

Z ing, Zack and have fun.

A panda is my favourite animal.

B e happy like I am always.

E ncourage people like I do.

L ive, laugh and love everyone.

L ike people's opinions, like I do.

A nd, I love to have fun.

Izabella Scheerova (8)

St Matthew's CE Primary School, West Wimbledon

Sport Is Fun

S upportive person, ready to pounce on the go, give me a shout.

P assionate, ready to ration it, captive but adaptive.

O ptician is a new addition.

R apid rockstar, ready to roar.

T eamwork makes the dream work.

Y ou work every day to have the best play.

Raphael Faponnle (8)

St Matthew's CE Primary School, West Wimbledon

Larissa, Me And Myself

L ikeable, loyal and lovely.
A ctive, adaptable and amiable.
R esponsible, reliable and relaxed.
I ntelligent, inspiring and important.
S ensible, superb and smart.
S incere, sporty and supportive.
A mazing, approachable and attentive.

Larissa De Campos-Michalowicz (8)

St Matthew's CE Primary School, West Wimbledon

Calla

C alla is a bright and wonderful child

A nd my favourite colour is pink and I

L ike going to the park and playing with my friends, I

L ike the cross country run because it helps to get fit

A nd I like PE the most because it is fun.

Calla Bliss Rayne (8)

St Matthew's CE Primary School, West Wimbledon

This Is Me

F riendly and fun, that's me

R eally, I'm good company

E xtremely hard-working

Y ou won't find me lurking

A s I do my homework with glee.

Freya Tamblyn (9)
St Matthew's CE Primary School, West Wimbledon

It's Okay

You know when the sun gives you a sunburn,
It's okay because you can add aloe wherever
it hurts.
You know when you spill something on you,
It's okay because you can wipe it off if it's small.
You know when you spill something on someone
accidentally,
It's okay because you can simply say sorry
And they will say it's okay.

You know when you fall,
It's okay because if you check where you got
hurt, and it doesn't hurt.
It's okay because you will be okay.
You know when you trip and it hurts,
It's okay because you can add a bandaid to
where it hurts.
You know when you trip someone by accident,
Just say sorry and they will say it's okay.
You know when you say sorry to someone,
You can relax yourself.
And always listen to your parents.

Holiness Amfo Nkrumab (7)
St Teresa's Catholic Primary School, Parkfields

Everyone Is Unique And Special

Some people are spoilt,
Some people are weak,
Some people are comparing themselves
to the poor,
Some people are in the war,
Some people are very important,
Some people are revenging,
Some people are homeless,
Some people are very very rich,
Some people are royalty,
But everyone is unique and special,
Everyone is also very important...
Maybe you're poor, maybe you're royalty,
maybe you're homeless
But everyone should love one another
as Christ loves his church.

Chikaima Ezekaka (7)
St Teresa's Catholic Primary School, Parkfields

This Is Me

This is me,
Sometimes I am happy,
Sometimes I am sad,
Sometimes I am lonely,
And sometimes I am mad.
Sometimes I am sick,
Sometimes I am healed,
Sometimes I am as colourful as a rainbow,
And sometimes I am pretty.
Sometimes I am as shimmering as a star.
Sometimes I am terrified.
Sometimes I am as bright as a moon,
And sometimes I am cheerful.
Everyone is special and we are kind,
We always have a smile on our faces,
And we care for each other.

Meagan Mazivanhanga (7)
St Teresa's Catholic Primary School, Parkfields

Always Be Obedient

Always listen to your parents,
Always listen to your teachers,
Always be obedient by taking out the trash,
Always tidy up your bed when you wake up,
Always do your homework after school,
Always be patient at school while doing your work.
I am always obedient by washing the dishes,
I am always obedient by following the rules,
Obedience is the key to greatness.

Ketochi Okenwa (7)
St Teresa's Catholic Primary School, Parkfields

Me

This is me.
I like pizza.
I like my school.
I like my teacher.
I like playing with my toys.
My dad likes to take me to the beach.
I play with my dad.
I like my best friend.
I love my house.
I like to play football.
I love my mum and dad.
I like to drink milkshakes.
I love Mum and Dad's house.
I like to go to Fun World.

Tajveer Kang (7)
St Teresa's Catholic Primary School, Parkfields

I'm Who I Am

I can sing,
I can dance,
I'm as beautiful as can be,
Now listen up everyone, you
can't be like me in a tree!
When I'm fun,
I'm in the sun,
I'd like a ball,
But it's too small,
I was in a dream,
About a stream,
When I'm cool,
I go and dive into the pool.

I am the best!

Talisha Linton (7)
St Teresa's Catholic Primary School, Parkfields

This Is Me!

I like sports.
But sometimes I am sad.
Sometimes I am happy.
I am kind to people.
I want to be a pro footballer.
I like to eat chicken nuggets.
I like to be helpful.
I like to eat pizza.
I can achieve anything.
I like reading books.
Sometimes I am excited.
This is me.
I always like to play football.

Marcus Nagy (7)
St Teresa's Catholic Primary School, Parkfields

Ice Cream School

Ice cream school has lots of ice cream,
It is the best, it has lots of flavours,
Coconut, strawberry, chocolate, vanilla
and caramel,
All ice cream is sweet and delish,
Every single bit of ice cream that you eat,
Has lots of grams of sugar,
When someone is sad,
Ice cream cheers them up.

Amelia Mehmi (7)
St Teresa's Catholic Primary School, Parkfields

Clever Boy

I am Enoch Shittu
I am a boy
I am seven years old
I am cute and a clever boy
I love maths
I can add. 10+10=20
I can minus. 20-10=10
I can read my times tables from 2 to 12
I can divide my numbers like
15÷3=5. 40÷10=4.

Enoch Shittu (7)

St Teresa's Catholic Primary School, Parkfields

The Things That I Like

I love my pet bear,
I love my lair,
I love my hair,
I love my chair.

I love drinks,
I love to get fired,
I love hats,
I love to get hired.

I love school,
I love bats,
I want a friend,
I want a hat.

Kendrick Dyoco (8)
St Teresa's Catholic Primary School, Parkfields

Ice School

The ice school has lots of yummy ice
cream and yummy cakes.
I like the school food.
I like the pizza at St Teresa's,
I love the sandwiches at St Teresa's,
I love ham sandwiches.

Lailena Madden
St Teresa's Catholic Primary School, Parkfields

I'm So Happy

Sometimes I'm so happy.
Sometimes I'm so angry.
Sometimes I'm so sad.
Sometimes I'm so sick.
Sometimes I'm so hungry.
Sometimes I'm surprised.

Krishiv Sharma (8)
St Teresa's Catholic Primary School, Parkfields

Kindness

I am as tall as a tree,
I am over the sky
I am as kind as a bee.
I am more clever than a rainbow.
Sometimes I am happy,
Sometimes I am sad.

Hasel Usieki (7)
St Teresa's Catholic Primary School, Parkfields

This Is Me And What I Love

David is my name
I love football
I like to ride my bike
I like to eat spaghetti
I love maths, science and art
I am happy
I love food.

David Lawal (7)
St Teresa's Catholic Primary School, Parkfields

Family

My mum and dad both love me
They help me grow into the best I can be
And then there's my cat!
He's so soft and cuddly!

Sara Williams (7)

St Teresa's Catholic Primary School, Parkfields

This Is Me

This is me
I am Tyrell
I like art
I like music
I like guitars
I like my classmates.

Tyrell Madden (7)
St Teresa's Catholic Primary School, Parkfields

Untitled

I am a jazzy JD dancing pupil.
I am a happy, dazzling, funny person.
I am a lover of Squishmallows.
I am as fast as a cheetah eating marshmallows.
I am in the Theatre School of Scotland Drama.
I am a total drama llama.
I am a blue-eye blondy.
I am a boba/bubble tea drink lover.
I want to be an actress when I'm older.
I am obsessed with watermelons.
I am not a fan of onions.
I am a popping pineapple person.
I am a good drawer.
I am a very good sport.
I am an amazing avocado eater.
I am a very good knitter.
This is me.

Millie McKay (9)
Whinhill Primary School, Greenock

Golf

One club, one ball, I used the club to hit the ball.
Tiger Woods can hit the ball as fast as a tiger.
Yet the ball can only go so far.
Every hole it could be a shot of 150 yards or
15 yards, it is hit or miss.
You must keep focusing on the ball.
I love the 8 iron as it is the best piece of kit.
Never drive a golf buggy over the putting green
as it could damage it.

Owen Porteous (9)
Whinhill Primary School, Greenock

Holidays

T here are hundreds of holidays

H undreds of holidays I've been on are good

I love chocolate and sweets on holiday, they are so good

S lopes are too steep for skiing

I love going on holiday

S uper skiing, go skiing

M y favourite thing to do is play Fortnite

E lves are small when I see them.

Thomas Robertson (7)
Whinhill Primary School, Greenock

My Role Model Unspeakable

U nspeakable is a gamer and he plays on a PC
N ot everyone knows him
S ecret to me
P atient and understanding
E specially with me
A wesome at building on Minecraft
K yle is his brother
A ble to survive a creeper
B ut he is so chatty
L oves Minecraft
E ats pizza all the time.

Ajay Mohan (8)
Whinhill Primary School, Greenock

![YoungWriters logo] YoungWriters Est. 1991

My Favourite Animal

C heetahs are as fast as a Lamborghini and a
   Ferrari.

H ere comes a cheetah to his house in the jungle.

E very one of them is fast.

E very one of them loves food.

T hey play with each other.

A rgh! The forest is falling down because the
   wood is getting cut down.

H ere are the cheetahs eating cheese sticks.

Evan Smillie (8)

Whinhill Primary School, Greenock

Likes And Dislikes

I am a
Kind person
Sporty person
Drama person
Playful person
Football person
Running person
Pineapple person
Chocolately person
Not an onion person
Not a smoking person
Not a beansprout person
Not an inside person
Not a cherry person
Not a raspberry person
This is me.

Cameron Marshall (9)
Whinhill Primary School, Greenock

This Is Me

T he most loving, kind person.
H ave many annoying people next to me.
I love my family and dog.
S chool and love ice cream.

I love my friends and dog.
S ometimes I make cookies.

M e and my dog chill.
E very day me and my family go out.

Kameron Morrison (8)
Whinhill Primary School, Greenock

My Favourite Thing

F rance was our topic last year.

O ur school is near my house.

O ne of our planets is creativity.

T his poem is for a competition.

B alls are in nearly every sport.

A re you in a sport?

L ocks can open with a key.

L amborghinis are as fast as a tiger.

Jake Barclay (8)
Whinhill Primary School, Greenock

My Favourite Thing To Do

F ebruary was very cold
O n Saturday, I went to football
O n Monday, I went to school
T uesday, I played with my dog
B eing annoying
A good team player
L ast Friday, I played FIFA 23
L iteracy is my favourite subject.

Noah Doherty (8)

Whinhill Primary School, Greenock

My Favourite Animal

This is a creature of the sky,
They like to be up high.

They are very protective,
I wouldn't go near it.

The Americans must be scared of them,
They fly free in America.

When it's night,
I don't think they are that bright.

Macey Quigg (9)
Whinhill Primary School, Greenock

All About Me

T he beach is one of my favourite places
H appy when I play football
I love my family so much
S ensible.

I am tall
S ometimes annoying.

M y house is big
E vie is my name.

Evie Jamieson (9)
Whinhill Primary School, Greenock

All About Me

My favourite colour is yellow.
I like chocolate cake.
I don't like Brussels sprouts.
I would like to live in a blue castle.
I am a fantastic footballer.
I love to run.
I am competitive.
I don't like heights.
I like birds.

Ikram Mashwani (9)
Whinhill Primary School, Greenock

This Is Me

I am a fantastic footballer
I am a marvellous midfielder
I am a great gamer
I am not a tuna person
I am not a cricket person
I am a music person
I am a friendly person
This is me.

Kian O'Shea (9)
Whinhill Primary School, Greenock

This Is Me

I am super fast like a cheetah.
I am very funny like a comedian.
I have blue eyes like the sky.
I have blonde hair like the beach.
This is me.

Blake McKinnon (9)
Whinhill Primary School, Greenock

This Is Me!

I am a kind, happy and organised person.

A zzaam is my obnoxious little brother
M y angelic little sister is called Dynwen

H annah Banana is my nickname
A cting is my passion, it's terrific fun
N ever give up, even if your life is a roller coaster like mine
N o one is like me, I am so unique
A nd when I get praised I feel like I've reached the highest peak
H aving heaps of happy times while hanging out with my friends makes my day, and it's the best.

Hannah Muhammad (10)
Ysgol Gymraeg Henllan, Henllan

This Is Me

J acob is my name,
A ll the time I dream about being a footballer,
C aring and charming like a cat,
O nions taste disgusting,
B eing with my family is the best.

R ich is what I want to be in the future,
O ne thing I fear is sharks,
B ut I love my family,
E d Sheeran is my favourite singer,
R oaring tigers are cool,
T igers are my favourite animal,
S kye and Storm are my pets.

Jacob Roberts (9)
Ysgol Gymraeg Henllan, Henllan

All About Me

I am a happy, funny and kind person.
I really love to swim like a fish.
I wish to be a strong swimmer.
I try to be good, but sometimes I get
angry when provoked.
I like to play the piano, I think I'm quite good.
I hate heights.
It makes me shiver with fright!
I dream day and night of being a gymnast
And I wonder every day, will I ever be
as good as the gymnasts on TV?
I love animals.
One day I'd like to have my own pet.

Efa Parkes (10)
Ysgol Gymraeg Henllan, Henllan

This Is Me!

H appy, friendly and a caring person
A rchie is my older brother
P umpkin pie I do not like
P enguins are my favourite animals
Y ear Six is the best year in school

P orridge is very tasty
E arrings, I love to wear
R oyalty is what I wish to be
S uperstar is what I want to be in the future
O ne and only Molly
N o one else like me.

Molly Lawson (10)
Ysgol Gymraeg Henllan, Henllan

All About Me!

A kind and funny person

L emonade is very nice

L eah is my lovely name

A wel is my youngest sister

B ut I don't like bolognese

O ut of the house is fun

U K is where I live

T ry my best on everything, you should too!

M y life is like a roller coaster sometimes

E ducation is what I learn in school.

Leah Jones (10)

Ysgol Gymraeg Henllan, Henllan

Football Mad

W rexham is the best team
R yan Reynolds would be proud
E very game is very tough
X -ray for when I'm injured
H eader the hard ball (*Bang!*)
A cademy scouts are after me
M aking money from my contract

A mazing atmosphere at the arena
F ocus on the game
C hanting loudly from the crowd.

Noa Evans (10)
Ysgol Gymraeg Henllan, Henllan

This Is Me Poem

I fan is my name
F un playing rugby
A round the merry-go-round
N ational schools rocks

H ide the ball and kick it into the hall
U nion Jack is the English flag
G o to the circus to see the clowns
H alloween is the scariest time of the year
E scape from a dark room
S weets are nice and yummy.

Ifan Hughes (9)
Ysgol Gymraeg Henllan, Henllan

This Is Me!

M an United is the best.

A nd they can beat all the rest.

N o, they can't lose.

U nited is gonna win the league.

N obody will stand a chance.

I love Man United.

T hey should win the team of the season.

E veryone will be destroyed by them.

D on't doubt Man United.

Azzaam Muhammad (9)

Ysgol Gymraeg Henllan, Henllan

This Is Me Poem

T his is my poem

H ard work is what I fear

I am a caring, compassionate and competitive person

S chool is what I love and learn new things

I wonder about the future

S ometimes I can have trouble with work

M y family and friends are my everything

E lizabeth is my name.

Elizabeth Vaughan Hepple (10)
Ysgol Gymraeg Henllan, Henllan

This Is Me

N eptune is my favourite planet.

E arth is where I was born.

V auxhall is a type of car.

I kicked the ball down the hall.

L ike playing football, it's my favourite sport.

L iverpool is the worst football team, in my opinion.

E aster is fun, having loads of chocolate.

Neville Headley (9)

Ysgol Gymraeg Henllan, Henllan

Fantastic Football

I finally flicked the football flying far,
Because I am a star, I fear Liverpool
beating Man United,
I'm a fantastic footballer like Ronaldo,
I finally scored my fifteenth goal,
Football is my favourite,
My family is fantastic and so supportive,
I hate it when the whistle blows so angrily.

Elis Smith (10)
Ysgol Gymraeg Henllan, Henllan

Acrostic Poem

E verton is my favourite football team.

V olkswagen is one of my favourite cars.

E lla is my little sister.

R acing cars is what I do.

T offee is the nickname of the team.

O ctober is my birth month.

N o, we did not get relegated.

Harvey Davies (11)

Ysgol Gymraeg Henllan, Henllan

This Is Me!

C hristmas is the best
E ating biscuits, burgers and chocolate is nice
N osebleeds aren't very good
W ales is where I was born
Y elling can get annoying
N ature looks pretty when I go walking.

Cenwyn Arman (9)

Ysgol Gymraeg Henllan, Henllan

About Me

A mazing at art.

B eing helpful is what I do.

O utstanding, I am.

U nique signature, I have.

T alented, I want to be.

M egan is my name.

E nergetic personality is what I have.

Megan J (9)

Ysgol Gymraeg Henllan, Henllan

Horses Are My Favourite

H orses are my favourite thing.
O pal only likes oats.
R unning up the garden like a rocket.
S illy, scary spiders.
E nergetically running with horses.
S carlett is my name, and I love horses.

Scarlett Jones (10)

Ysgol Gymraeg Henllan, Henllan

YOUNG WRITERS INFORMATION

We hope you have enjoyed reading this book – and that you will continue to in the coming years.

If you're the parent or family member of an enthusiastic poet or story writer, do visit our website **www.youngwriters.co.uk/subscribe** and sign up to receive news, competitions, writing challenges and tips, activities and much, much more! There's lots to keep budding writers motivated!

If you would like to order further copies of this book, or any of our other titles, then please give us a call or order via your online account.

Young Writers
Remus House
Coltsfoot Drive
Peterborough
PE2 9BF
(01733) 890066
info@youngwriters.co.uk

Join in the conversation!
Tips, news, giveaways and much more!

 **YoungWritersUK**    **YoungWritersCW**    **youngwriterscw**

Scan me to watch the
This Is Me video!